GW00771938

Short Stack Editions | Volume 14

Prosciutto di Parma

by Sara Jenkins

Short Stack Editions

Publisher: Nick Fauchald
Creative Director: Rotem Raffe
Editor: Kaitlyn Goalen
Copy Editor: Abby Tannenbaum
Director of Development: Mackenzie Smith

ISBN 978-0-9907853-3-0

Printed in New York City
March 2015

Table of Contents

Fat

Scraps

We'll be honest: Before working on this book, prosciutto di Parma had a limited presence in our kitchen. We'd spring for the high-end ham when assembling a fancy cheese plate or making a classic chicken saltimbocca, but that was about it.

Then came the recipes of Sara Jenkins, who gives prosciutto di Parma its due in various forms and functions at both her restaurants and at home. Part of Jenkins's casual intimacy with the ingredient is the product of upbringing: She spent several years of her childhood in Italy, where prosciutto di Parma is a regular item on any grocery list. Accordingly, several of the recipes in this edition skew toward the flavors of prosciutto's homeland and the author's youth.

But Jenkins, whose resume includes stints at some of New York City's top restaurants, including two of her own, is not boxed in by nostalgia. Her keen palate and unique style have led to entirely new considerations of prosciutto di Parma, drawing a much larger culinary map. Tacos, it turns out, make an awesome vehicle for this deeply flavored ham.

What's more, Jenkins springs prosciutto from the precious handcuffs of the antipasto plate. For every recipe that calls for delicate sheets of perfectly sliced ham, there's another that unceremoniously but deliciously uses scraps or thick-cut rustic hunks.

As a result, this edition is a justification as much as it is a celebration: It explains and validates prosciutto di Parma's vaunted reputation as one of the great ingredients in the world.

—*The Editors*

Introduction

I grew up in Italy, so prosciutto has always been part of my gastronomic landscape. I have vivid memories of my neighbor bracing a home-style, air-cured ham against her chest while she sawed off thick slivers. She'd drape them over slices of sweet cantaloupe, picked that morning in her garden before the sun got too hot.

But for prosciutto di Parma, we'd have to go to our neighborhood *alimentari*, where the counter man would expertly slice paper-thin sheets of the prized ham. We'd pair the slices with the freshest milky mozzarella or layer them onto bubbling hot pizza as it came out of the wood-burning oven. It tasted so different from my neighbor's rustic meat: It virtually melted in your mouth and held a delicate balance between sweet and salty without either overpowering the other.

I quickly learned that prosciutto crudo ("raw" ham) was the generic term for a salt-and-air-cured ham. And indeed, salt-cured ham is nothing new; it's an ancient practice, and different cultures, from Spain to the American South, have their variations. Prosciutto crudo as made in Italy is a whole hind leg of a pig, cured in salt for a specified number of days, then rinsed, cleaned, seasoned and hung to dry in an airy and cold environment. But prosciutto di Parma refers to something quite specific: These hams come from single region (Parma) and follow strict guidelines set forth and controlled by a consortium. Everything from what the pig eats (which includes scraps and whey from the nearby Parmigiano-Reggiano cheese production) to how the ham is cured is

highly specified, resulting in a superior ingredient known around the globe.

In the United States, prosciutto di Parma is usually something you find on restaurant menus rather than in home kitchens, but let me assure you that prosciutto has plenty of applications in your cooking repertoire. In Italian kitchens, a leg of prosciutto is a workhorse, used over time and in a multitude of ways until every last bit of the ham is used.

The simplest and most common way to enjoy prosciutto is to slice it thin and pair it with sweet fruit (such as cantaloupe or figs) or something mild and creamy such as mozzarella cheese. In addition, there are endless ways to cook with prosciutto di Parma. I've watched cooks in Umbria save the fat from the trimmings and pound it with herbs to coat and baste a rack of lamb. The bone makes an amazing flavoring agent for broths and soups, while the scraps of the end piece can boost the flavor of ragù for pasta.

You can also use prosciutto in the same traditional ways that country ham is used here in the States, with grits and pan gravy, or even to jazz up Asian-style stir-fried rice. Any place you might use a cured ham, prosciutto di Parma will work just as well—often better.

Some of these recipes are things I have made my whole cooking life; others are brand-new ideas. Please feel free to make substitutions as needed to match your mood and larder: With the exception of baking, nothing will be ruined if you don't have exactly the same ingredients I called for.

Because of its guaranteed high quality, prosciutto di Parma is a cook's best friend: Whether it's the unadulterated centerpiece of a plate or part of a more elaborate dish, the ham raises any dish up to its excellent standards.

—Sara Jenkins

Recipes

Sourcing and Storing Prosciutto

Picking Your Ham

I believe that a ham takes many months of aging to really come to fruition and develop all of its flavor; plus, the older the ham is, the easier it is to slice. In America, you'll find prosciutto di Parma in a range of ages, most often 14 to 16 months, which will do the trick for most of the recipes in this book. But in recipes that really benefit from that mature flavor, I've called for 24-month ham, which is my preferred aging. If you can't find 24-month ham, buy the most-aged one you can find.

How to Buy

Traditionally, every farmer in Italy would have a few hams swinging from a rafter in the attic all year, pulling one down to carve off bits as needed. But since most of us aren't Italian farmers, it's more likely you'll buy your prosciutto from a gourmet deli or Italian food store. Look at the deli counter first and get freshly sliced whenever you can. If presliced is your only option, look for the Parma crown on the package to ensure you're getting the real thing.

Shop from a place where a counter person can slice the ham in front of you. It requires special skill to slice the prosciutto on a machine to get even, perfectly marbled slices, and it's worth seeking out someone who cares about doing it correctly.

Some recipes call for large hunks of unsliced ham, prosciutto scraps or even the bone. These can usually be purchased anywhere that slices its hams to order—just ask!

Whole Hams

If you're feeling ambitious (or channeling your inner Italian farmer) and want your own ham hanging around, you'll need a few tools of the trade: a ham stand and a long, thin, slicing knife (like one you'd use to carve lox). Store the prosciutto in a cold and airy room; cellars are great if you're lucky enough to have one. As you carve your prosciutto, save any of the fatty bits that you trim to use when you cook.

If you don't have your own ham and stand at home, there's nothing wrong with getting your prosciutto sliced for you at the shop. Every deli or grocery store in Italy has a slicer that is used to shave prosciutto every day for the millions of Italians who don't have a ham at home. When I lived in Italy, picking up sliced prosciutto at the *alimentari* and a ripe cantaloupe at the market nearby was the best way to make a quick and dazzling lunch for anyone who happened to drop in.

Storing Your Ham

Unless you're using a whole ham, buy just as much prosciutto as you need and store it in the refrigerator. As it sits in the fridge, the prosciutto gets harder and harder to separate into the beautiful individual slices it came in; while it's still perfectly delicious and edible, it's not going to fan out across the plate as nicely. Scraps of fat or the heel of the prosciutto can be tightly wrapped in plastic and stored in the freezer for a couple of months to dig out when you need it.

Pizza with Spicy Peach Jam, Burrata & Prosciutto

Growing up in Rome, one of my favorite pizzas was a classic Margherita that had prosciutto crudo draped over it just as it came out of the oven. This is a more sophisticated take, topped with creamy, soft burrata and peach jam that's been livened up with a hot chile. The dough is an adaption of famed *pizzaiolo* Gabriele Bonci's dough. In my many years of making pizza, it is hands down the best dough-making technique I've ever come across. For baking a great pizza at home, it does really help to have a stone or baking steel, but don't be dissuaded if all you have is a sheet pan. This pizza will still be delicious.

Spicy Peach Jam

4 to 6 super-ripe fragrant peaches

Juice from 1 lemon

1 spicy chile, such as habanero, whole

¼ cup sugar

Peel the peaches and cut into chunks, discarding the pits. Place the peach chunks in a large bowl and toss with the lemon juice so they don't discolor. In a heavy-bottomed saucepan over low heat, add the peaches and chile and cook gently until the peaches begin to fall apart, about 20 minutes. Add the sugar and cook until it has dissolved and the peaches have broken down. Remove the chile and discard. Let the jam cool, then transfer to a lidded container and refrigerate until ready to use. This jam will keep at least a month in the fridge or up to 6 months frozen.

Pizza Dough

8 cups (2 pounds) all-purpose flour

3 teaspoons active dry yeast

3 cups (1 pound 8 ounces) water

3 tablespoons olive oil

1 teaspoon sea salt

(Start the dough the day before you want pizza.) In a large bowl, mix the flour and yeast together. Add the water and stir together with a wooden spoon until the mixture begins to form a dough. Stir in the oil and salt. Cover with a kitchen towel and let rise until doubled, about 1 hour.

When the dough has doubled, take it out of the bowl and place on a lightly floured work surface. Using your fingers, spread the dough out into a rectangular shape about 2 inches thick. Pick up two ends and fold them over into the middle as though you're folding up a letter. Turn the folded dough 90 degrees and repeat two or three times, rotating the dough after every fold. Return the dough to the bowl and let it rest for another 15 minutes or so, then repeat the folding and resting again. Repeat the folding and resting at least three more times and up to six for optimal results. When you've finished folding and resting the dough, return it to the bowl and cover with plastic wrap. Refrigerate overnight.

Assembling the Pizza

1 Pizza Dough

1 pound burrata

¼ cup olive oil, divided

⅓ cup grated Parmigiano-Reggiano cheese, divided

About ½ cup Spicy Peach Jam

16 to 20 paper-thin slices 24-month-aged prosciutto di Parma, divided

2 scallions, cut into slivers (optional), divided

When you're ready to bake the pizza, preheat the oven (with a pizza stone or steel, if using) to its maximum temperature, most likely 500°. Divide the dough into four pieces and form each into a loose ball. Cover the balls with a lightly floured cloth and let rest for 20 minutes.

Using your fingers, form one of the dough balls into a flattened disc, about 8 inches in diameter, and place on a pizza paddle (if you plan to cook on a pizza stone) or baking sheet. Divide the burrata into quarters. Tear one of the quarters into pieces and scatter them over the dough. Drizzle with 1 tablespoon of oil and sprinkle with some of the grated Parmigiano-Reggiano. Dot a few tablespoons of the spicy jam in the bare spaces between the cheese, but be shy with it.

Transfer the pizza to the stone or steel, if using, or transfer the baking sheet to the oven, and bake until the dough is crisp and golden and the cheese is bubbling and melted. When the hot pizza comes out, drape it with 4 or 5 slices of prosciutto, a quarter of the scallions, if using, and cut into slices. Repeat with remaining pizzas and serve.

Wilted Greens with Prosciutto

Pairing greens with cured pork is a classic combination all over the world, and I never tire of this Mediterranean take, which dresses humble, hearty greens with rich and luxurious prosciutto. This is a very easy dish to make, but the timing is everything: You want to lay the prosciutto slices over the greens while they're still warm, which will gently wilt the ham and start to melt the fat. To turn this side dish into a starter, place a mound of the greens on grilled or toasted bread.

¼ cup plus 2 tablespoons extra-virgin olive oil, divided

2 garlic cloves, smashed

1 red onion, halved lengthwise and sliced into thin half moons

1 small dried hot chile, such as chile de árbol

8 cups mixed baby cooking greens

Sea salt and freshly ground black pepper

1 lemon, halved

12 very thin slices of prosciutto di Parma

serves
·4·

In a large heavy-bottomed skillet, heat the ¼ cup of oil over low heat. Add the garlic and gently fry until it's lightly golden on both sides. Add the onion and cook until it begins to soften. Add the chile, followed by the greens. Turn up the heat to medium-high and toss with tongs until the greens just begin to wilt.

Remove the pan from the heat and, working quickly, divide the greens among four plates. Season with salt and pepper, a squeeze of fresh lemon and the remaining 2 tablespoons of oil. Lay the prosciutto slices over the greens, covering them in a single layer, 3 slices per plate. Serve immediately.

Cantaloupe Soup
with Prosciutto Crostini

This is a fancy reconstruction of the classic prosciutto and melon appetizer that you'll find throughout Italy in the summer months. The sweetness of the cantaloupe pairs beautifully with the salty complexity of a well-aged prosciutto di Parma. I love to serve this as a passed appetizer for an outdoor party or event; I lay the toast over the top of the glass so you can walk and sip and nibble all at the same time.

1 ripe cantaloupe, divided

1 medium cucumber, peeled and cut into 2-inch cubes

1 shallot, diced

Sea salt

3 tablespoons sherry vinegar

1 cup plain yogurt

⅓ cup extra-virgin olive oil

1 stick (½ cup) unsalted butter, at room temperature

8 slices crusty bread

8 paper-thin slices 24-month-aged prosciutto di Parma

serves
-4-

Halve the melon and scoop out the seeds. Set aside one of the halves; peel and dice the other half, and place the flesh in the bowl of a food processor. Add the cucumber, shallot and a pinch of salt and puree. Add the vinegar and puree until smooth. Add the yogurt and pulse a few times to combine. With the motor running, add the oil in a slow and steady stream. Transfer the soup to a bowl and chill for at least 2 hours and up to overnight. (If the soup separates a bit overnight, just give it a whisk to recombine.)

Remove the peel from the other half of the cantaloupe and cut the flesh into chunks. In a food processor, puree the melon with the butter, letting it run for about 10 minutes to really blend the two ingredients. When the melon butter turns a beautiful salmon color and is completely combined, spoon it out onto a roll of parchment paper and roll it up like a log. Transfer the butter to the refrigerator and chill until firm, at least 2 hours.

To serve, toast the bread slices until barely golden. Spread a bit of the melon butter over each piece of toast, then top with a piece of the prosciutto. Pour the soup into small glasses so your guests can sip it without a spoon. Serve the melon soup with the toast.

Saltimbocca alla Romana

Saltimbocca is perhaps the most iconic way to cook with prosciutto in the Italian cooking canon, and with good reason: It's quick, easy and delicious. The original recipe calls for thin veal cutlets, but can just as easily be made with pork or chicken. Because this is such a beloved dish, everyone has his or her own method and insists that it's the most authentic. In my version, the prosciutto is on the outside of the meat, so it can crisp up with the sage leaf, which adds texture as well as flavor to the dish. I add the dried chile because it's delicious, though inauthentic; no Roman would stand for it.

1½ pounds veal cutlets (you can substitute chicken or pork cutlets)

¼ pound thinly sliced prosciutto di Parma

1 bunch sage

All-purpose flour, for dredging

serves 4

2 to 3 tablespoons extra-virgin olive oil, divided

2 tablespoons butter, divided

Freshly ground black pepper

1 dried hot chile, such as chile de árbol

½ cup dry white wine

Lay the veal cutlets on a cutting board and pound out lightly to ¼-inch thickness. Top each cutlet evenly with a slice or two of prosciutto. Place 2 sage leaves on top of the prosciutto, one on each end of the cutlet. Repeat for all the cutlets. Use toothpicks to pin the sage leaves and prosciutto onto the cutlets. Dredge the cutlets with flour.

Heat 2 tablespoons of the oil and 1 tablespoon of the butter in a large skillet over medium-high heat. Add the cutlets, prosciutto-side down, sprinkle with pepper and cook until browned on one side, about 2 minutes. Turn and cook until the other side is browned, about 2 minutes more, adding an additional tablespoon of oil if necessary. Transfer the veal to a platter.

Crumble the chile between your fingers and add it to the pan, then add the wine and use a wooden spoon to scrape up any browned bits that stick to the bottom of the pan. Add any juices from the resting veal and cook until the liquid starts to thicken, about 4 minutes. Add the remaining tablespoon of butter and stir until melted. Pour the sauce over the veal and serve.

Prosciutto with Pears & St-Marcellin Cheese

One of the best things about prosciutto di Parma is that the most delicious preparations also tend to be the simplest. Sweet fruit is a classic pairing for the sweet and nutty ham, while adding a creamy, rich cheese like St-Marcellin from France only heightens the flavors more. If you can't find St-Marcellin, feel free to substitute another creamy, fresh cheese or something that tastes extra buttery. An artisan Italian robiola would do well, as would a stellar Brie, but we rarely find the latter in the U.S.

18 paper-thin slices 24-month-aged prosciutto di Parma

4 to 6 ripe pears

2 wheels St-Marcellin or similar cheese (about 4 ounces each)

12 pieces toasted bread

Extra-virgin olive oil

Freshly ground black pepper

serves
6

Arrange three slices of prosciutto on each of six plates. Quarter and core the pears and divide among the plates. Slice the cheese into triangles and divide among the plates, or if the cheese is super-ripe, scoop spoonfuls onto each plate. Pile a couple of pieces of toast on each plate. Finish by drizzling oil and cracking some fresh pepper over everything.

Prosciutto & Buffalo Mozzarella

Everyone loves buffalo mozzarella with fresh tomato and basil, the Neapolitan dish known as *insalata caprese*. But what do the Neapolitans do in winter, when the tomatoes aren't that tasty? They substitute sweet, salty prosciutto for the tomatoes to make the dish a year-round affair. This recipe relies on finding the best possible ingredients; most of your prep work is in the shopping. You want to use the best, freshest buffalo mozzarella you can find and a well-balanced aged prosciutto di Parma sliced paper-thin.

1 pound just-landed-from-Italy buffalo mozzarella, ideally in two balls

8 to 12 paper-thin slices 24-month-aged prosciutto di Parma

A handful of wild arugula (optional)

Freshly ground black pepper

¼ cup high-quality extra-virgin olive oil

Grilled bread, for serving

serves
-4-

The mozzarella will have a seam. Cut the balls in half by cutting perpendicular to the seam. Cut each half in half again. Place two pieces of mozzarella on each plate and lay 3 to 4 slices of prosciutto next to it. If you're using the arugula, place a little tangle between the cheese and the prosciutto. Crack a little black pepper over the cheese and drizzle the oil over the plate. Serve with grilled bread or toast to mop up the milky juices of the cheese.

Prosciutto-Wrapped Persimmons

When we harvest olives at my family's farm in Italy, persimmon season is often just starting up. We always have leftover olive oil from 1 or even 2 harvests ago, and it's a great opportunity to fry using extra-virgin olive oil, which is one of the most flavorful (and luxurious) fats to fry in. Fruit and prosciutto are frequently paired together raw; uniting them in the presence of a little heat is a less-expected but absolutely delicious tactic.

1 cup all-purpose flour

1½ cups club soda or seltzer

3 cups extra-virgin olive oil, for frying

3 to 4 fuyu persimmons

12 very thin slices prosciutto di Parma

Sea salt

serves 4 to 6

Make the batter: Add the flour to a large bowl and whisk in the club soda. Let the mixture rest for 30 minutes to allow the flour to absorb all the water it can. After 30 minutes, check and adjust the consistency of the batter by adding a pinch more flour or a bit more club soda, if needed. The consistency should be slightly thinner than Elmer's glue.

Heat the oil in a large heavy-bottomed pot until it reaches 360° to 365° on a deep-fry thermometer. Slice the persimmons into quarters and wrap each one with a piece of prosciutto. Dip the prosciutto-wrapped slices in batter and fry two or three pieces at a time so that the oil temperature remains constant. As the batter turns golden on one side, flip the pieces over and fry the other side. Transfer to a paper-towel-lined plate to drain and sprinkle with sea salt. Repeat until all of the persimmon pieces have been fried. Serve immediately.

Grits with Prosciutto & Gravy

Grits with country ham and pan gravy is a classic Southern dish. But using prosciutto di Parma instead makes it that much more elegant. Grits remind me of polenta, a dish I disdained as a child growing up in Italy for its extreme plainness. But when my friend "Hoppin'" John Taylor taught me to make grits this way, serving it with the classic ham and gravy, my entire outlook on the dish changed, and, by proxy, my feelings about polenta. Grits should be made with the best stone-ground corn you can find; Anson Mills is a good choice. The grind gives a pleasing rough texture and the artisan grain is packed with flavor.

For the grits:

Sea salt

2 tablespoons butter

1 cup stone-ground grits

For the ham and gravy:

10 ounces thickly sliced (about ¼ inch) prosciutto di Parma

¼ cup extra-virgin olive oil

2 tablespoons all-purpose flour

½ cup sherry

½ cup chicken stock (preferably homemade)

½ cup heavy cream

2 tablespoons freshly cracked black pepper

½ cup grated Parmigiano-Reggiano cheese

½ cup chopped flat-leaf parsley

Make the grits: In a large pot, bring 4 cups of water, with a pinch of salt and the butter, to a boil. Reduce the mixture to a simmer and add the grits, whisking constantly. Cook, stirring frequently, for 20 to 40 min-

utes. If the grits become so thick that they're hard to stir, add 2 table-spoons of water; repeat the addition of 2 tablespoons of water at a time as necessary. The grits are done when they're creamy and have lost their "crunch." Keep the grits warm over very low heat.

Make the ham and gravy: Cut the prosciutto slices into 1-inch wide strips. In a cast-iron skillet, heat the oil and fry the prosciutto slices on one side until they're browned and crisp. Transfer the prosciutto to a paper-towel-lined plate and set aside.

Remove all but ¼ cup of the fat and return the skillet to the heat. Add the flour to the pan and cook over low heat, stirring constantly, until it has browned in the residual fat and smells toasty, about 5 minutes. Stir in the sherry and let cook until the liquid has been absorbed. Add the stock and whisk until the mixture is smooth and thick. Add the cream and cook, stirring, until the sauce has reduced down to 1 cup. Stir in the black pepper.

Ladle the grits into bowls and top with a few spoonfuls of the gravy. Finish with a few strips of crispy prosciutto. Dust with Parmigiano-Reggiano and parsley and serve immediately.

Spinach Salad with Prosciutto Vinaigrette & Egg Mimosa

The French are fond of dressing dark greens with a warm bacon dressing, using the bacon fat to slick the greens, but I prefer the less aggressive flavor of prosciutto di Parma. At Manhattan's Union Square Greenmarket, you can buy the most intense baby spinach when it's in season. It's robust and very flavorful and stands up well to the crispy prosciutto and hard-boiled eggs in this salad dressing. Bagged baby spinach can be used as a substitute, of course, but if you can get to a farmers' market, I encourage you to seek out tender small spinach from a local grower. Here's a prep tip: Store your freshly washed salad greens in a damp cloth in the refrigerator for about an hour before you use them. As a result, they'll be even crisper on the plate despite the addition of the heavy dressing.

For the dressing:

½ cup extra-virgin olive oil, divided

½ cup diced prosciutto di Parma (I like using batons with plenty of fat attached, about 1 inch long by ¼ inch wide)

2 shallots, minced

1 tablespoon finely chopped herbs, such as thyme or marjoram

¼ cup young (2-year-old) balsamic vinegar

For the salad:

5 ounces baby spinach— trimmed, washed and dried

2 hard-boiled eggs, shells removed

serves -4-

Place a skillet over medium heat and add 2 tablespoons of oil and the prosciutto. When the prosciutto starts to crisp, add the shallots and

cook gently until they're softened and beginning to brown. Add the herbs and cook, stirring, for 1 or 2 minutes. Add the vinegar and simmer briskly for 5 minutes. Add the rest of the oil and keep the mixture warm.

Arrange the spinach in a bowl or on a platter. Place a mesh sieve over a cutting board and press the hard-boiled eggs through the sieve with a spoon to produce a fine crumble that resembles spring mimosa blossoms. To serve, drizzle the warm dressing over the spinach, then sprinkle with the crumbled egg and eat immediately.

Egg Tagliolini with Prosciutto, Butter & Parmesan

This dish is unabashedly simple—just pasta, butter, prosciutto and cheese—which provides an ideal forum for the prosciutto's flavor to really stand out. The goal here is not to get the prosciutto crispy, but to just gently steep it in the butter to pull out the maximum amount of flavor and nuance. This is a pretty easy dish to throw together and so worth it to spend the time making the pasta yourself (it's a great intro for homemade-pasta novices).

A note on the yield: Italians tend to eat a smaller portion of pasta as a course during the meal, while Americans like to eat it as their main dish. I find a pound of pasta serves six as a smaller Italian-style course but only four people if it's the main part of the meal.

For the tagliolini:

1 pound all-purpose flour

10 egg yolks

5 whole eggs

2 tablespoons olive oil

serves 4 to 6

For the dish:

6 tablespoons good-quality butter

¼ pound prosciutto di Parma, cut into ¼-inch-thick lardons

¼ cup grated Parmigiano-Reggiano cheese

Sea salt and freshly ground black pepper

Make the tagliolini: Place the flour in a food processor and, with the motor running, add the yolks and whole eggs, one at a time. The dough will be crumbly and a little granular, but it should hold together if you pinch it. Transfer the dough to a smooth work surface and knead it a few times. When the dough is smooth and has come together, rub the oil over the exterior of the dough and knead a few more times. Wrap the dough with plastic wrap and let rest for at least 15 minutes.

Cut the dough into three pieces, and wrap two in plastic wrap and set aside. Dust the remaining piece of dough with a little bit of flour and pat it out into a roughly rectangular shape. Run it through the widest setting on the pasta roller, then dust lightly with flour and roll it through the next thinnest setting. Repeat until you're two settings away from the thinnest setting. Repeat with the remaining two pieces of dough.

Cut the pasta sheets into 12-inch lengths. Set the pasta machine with the "tagliolini" cutter (the smallest cutter attachment with teeth that are about ⅛ inch wide), and run each sheet through. Toss the noodles with a little flour and let dry them on a wire rack until you're ready to cook.

If you don't have a pasta roller, you can roll the dough out with a straight (not tapered) rolling pin. Cut the dough into thirds, as you would with the pasta roller. Dust a large wooden surface with flour. Roll each piece of dough out to a uniform thinness and let dry for a few minutes. Gently fold the dough over itself and slice into ⅛-thick ribbons with a sharp knife and set aside.

Melt the butter in a large skillet over low heat and add the prosciutto. Gently cook without crisping the prosciutto or letting the butter brown. You want to just gently infuse the butter with the prosciutto.

Meanwhile, fill a large pot with salted water (we always say that you should add enough salt so that the water tastes of the sea). Bring the water to a boil and ladle 1 cup of the boiling water into the serving bowl to warm it up. Pour the water out, then add the prosciutto butter to the warm bowl.

Cook the pasta until it floats, 3 to 4 minutes (if you're using dry pasta, cook it according to the package instructions). Working quickly, scoop the pasta out of the water and transfer it to the serving bowl, stirring to coat it with the butter and prosciutto. Add the Parmigiano and toss some more. Season with salt and lots of freshly cracked black pepper. Serve immediately.

Stir-Fried Rice with Prosciutto

Stir-fried rice is one of those easy, clean-out-the-fridge Sunday supper kind of dishes that I love for its sheer flexibility. A little cured meat, a little fresh seafood, an egg, some greens and some leftover cooked rice come together to form an awesome meal. Truth be told, I often make extra rice so I can stir-fry it later. Although it might not seem obvious to use Italian prosciutto di Parma in a Chinese stir-fry dish, the flavor and texture work beautifully. The prosciutto crisps up, and the salty flavor punctuates the shrimp and rice.

5 tablespoons sesame cooking oil, divided

3 ounces thickly sliced prosciutto di Parma, cut into ¼-inch fat-streaked batons

3 garlic cloves, halved

1-inch piece of ginger, peeled and cut into slivers

12 fresh shiitake mushroom caps (about 5 ounces), diced

1 hot dried chile, such as chile de árbol

½ pound shrimp, peeled and cut into bite-size pieces

4 tablespoons sherry

2 eggs

Sea salt and freshly ground black pepper

¼ cup chopped cilantro, plus additional sprigs for garnish

2 tablespoons fish sauce or soy sauce

3 cups cooked jasmine rice

4 cups tatsoi or baby bok choy

4 scallions, cut into 2-inch pieces on the bias

2 to 3 tablespoons toasted sesame seeds

2 limes, cut into wedges

serves
-4-

Heat 2 tablespoons of oil in a large cast-iron pan over medium heat. Add the prosciutto, garlic and ginger. Add the mushroom caps and stir-fry,

stirring constantly, for a few minutes. Add the chile, shrimp and sherry and cook just until the shrimp are cooked through, 2 to 3 minutes. Transfer to a bowl and set aside.

Wipe out the pan, return to medium heat and add the remaining 3 tablespoons of oil. In a small bowl, beat the eggs with a little salt and pepper, ¼ cup chopped cilantro and the fish sauce. Add the rice to the pan and let it cook for a few minutes without stirring so that it crisps up slightly. Add the eggs and toss, then add the reserved shrimp mixture. Add the tatsoi and stir, cooking just until the greens begin to wilt. Stir in the scallions and the sesame seeds.

To serve, divide among plates and serve with additional cilantro sprigs and lime wedges for garnishing.

Cheesy Prosciutto Bread

This rich bread is frequently served around Easter in Italy's Umbrian Hills, probably as a welcome luxury following the lean fasting days of Lent. Be sure to use Tuscan pecorino, not Romano; the taste is more balanced and less aggressive than the better-known version. This is delicious lightly toasted with a little sweet butter or even the cantaloupe butter on page 16. It makes a rich and hearty breakfast, but it's also wonderful as an afternoon snack paired with a glass of crisp white wine and some olives.

2 tablespoons active dry yeast

1 cup of milk

10 eggs, beaten

2¾ cups grated pecorino Toscano

¾ cup (3½ ounces) diced Fontina cheese

1 cup (about 6 ounces) diced prosciutto di Parma

¼ teaspoon nutmeg

¼ cup extra-virgin olive oil

1 teaspoon sea salt

2 tablespoons freshly ground black pepper

4 cups all-purpose flour, divided

Butter, for greasing the pan

In a small bowl, combine the yeast and milk and let the mixture sit for 5 minutes so the yeast can bloom. Add the eggs, pecorino, Fontina, prosciutto, nutmeg, oil, salt and pepper. Add two cups of the flour and mix to form a wet dough, then add the remaining flour ½ a cup at a time, folding and stirring with a rubber spatula after each addition.

Divide the dough into two equal balls and transfer to two well-buttered loaf pans. Let rise until the dough has doubled in volume. I like to let

them rise slowly in the refrigerator overnight for the best flavor development, but if you're in a hurry, you can set them in a warm spot in your kitchen for a minimum of 2 hours.

Preheat the oven to 375°. Transfer the pans to the oven and bake for at least 1 hour or until the crust is golden and the loaf pulls away from the edges of the pan. Transfer to a wire rack and let cool in the pan for about 45 minutes before slicing and serving. The bread is best eaten within 2 days, or it can be wrapped in plastic and frozen for up to 1 month.

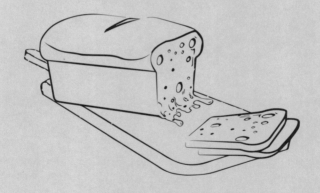

Potted & Deviled Prosciutto

I love the heat of Southern deviled ham but prefer the butterfat of traditional British potted ham, so I combined the best of both worlds here. The older the ham the better (this is a good opportunity to use up the end bit of a whole prosciutto). Serve these with pickles and toast for the perfect snack. Add a salad and it becomes a quick meal.

2 sticks (½ pound) unsalted butter

1 pound 24-month-aged prosciutto di Parma

1 tablespoon cider vinegar

1 shallot, finely diced

2 teaspoons brown mustard seeds

1 tablespoon harissa or other chile paste

¼ cup finely chopped parsley

1 tablespoon finely chopped thyme leaves

serves
·6·

Melt the butter in a medium heavy-bottomed saucepan over low heat to clarify it, spooning off the milk solids that rise to the top.

Meanwhile, shred or finely chop the prosciutto and add it to a medium bowl. Fold in the vinegar, shallot, mustard seeds, harissa, parsley and thyme. Mix gently. Add two thirds of the clarified butter and mix again. Divide the mixture among 6 individual 4-ounce ramekins or one large one, packing it down to fill all the crevices.

Cover the surface with a thin layer of the reserved clarified butter to seal. Refrigerate overnight before serving. The potted prosciutto can be covered and refrigerated for up to a week.

Prosciutto Fat-Crusted Rack of Lamb

In Umbria, local cooks save the fat trimmings from their prosciutto and then grind them up with an aromatic mix of savory herbs (such as rosemary, sage, bay leaf and wild fennel pollen). Smeared over a rack of lamb, the fat and herbs baste and protect the meat as it roasts. Roasting the whole rack is easy and looks very elegant when you present it at the table.

2 garlic cloves

1 sprig each rosemary, sage and marjoram

3 sprigs thyme

1 bay leaf

1 tablespoon fennel pollen (optional)

1 tablespoon freshly ground black pepper

8 ounces prosciutto di Parma fat (about 1 cup), finely chopped

1 cleaned 8-rib rack of lamb (about 2 pounds)

Sea salt

serves
·4·

Preheat the oven to 450°. In a food processor, pulse the garlic, rosemary, sage, marjoram, thyme, bay leaf, fennel pollen and pepper until finely chopped. Add the fat and puree until the fat is completely broken down and creamy. Transfer the mixture to a small bowl and chill in the freezer for 10 minutes or so to set it up.

Smear the fat all over the exterior of the lamb and place the rack in a roasting pan. Season liberally with sea salt and roast for 15 minutes. Turn the oven down to 325° and cook for 30 to 40 minutes longer or until a meat thermometer registers 130° to 140° for rare to medium rare. Let the roast rest for 15 minutes before carving and serving.

Salmon with Prosciutto-Cider Broth

I first tasted wild Atlantic salmon in Spain many years ago, and even now I'm haunted by the depth of its flavor. Atlantic salmon has an unctuous fattiness that's missing from Pacific salmon. But alas: Wild Atlantic salmon is sadly rare these days, so this recipe is my attempt to reverse engineer its potency. Prosciutto, added in two forms, is the secret key to creating a facsimile of that wild Atlantic salmon flavor; the fat and funk of the ham enrobe the fish in a meaty richness. When I close my eyes and take a bite, it's almost as good as the original. Almost.

---

2 pounds skin-on salmon fillet cut into 4 equal portions (I recommend high-quality organic farm-raised salmon)

Sea salt and freshly ground black pepper

4 ounces prosciutto di Parma fat

1 leek, cleaned and cut into ¼-inch dice

2 cups hard cider

2 cups chicken stock, preferably homemade

2 tablespoons cider vinegar

¼ cup clarified butter

8 thin slices 24-month-aged prosciutto di Parma

¼ cup parsley leaves

serves
-4-

Rinse the salmon fillets and pat them dry. Place the salmon, skin-side up, on a foil-lined roasting pan. Season the skin generously with salt and pepper.

In a food processor, grind the prosciutto fat to a rough paste, then transfer to a heavy-bottomed saucepan set over low heat. Slowly cook the fat until it is rendered, then add the leek and cook gently until it's wilted

and translucent. Add the hard cider and bring to a simmer to cook off the alcohol, 4 to 5 minutes. Add the chicken stock and reduce until only 2 cups of liquid remain, then add the vinegar. Keep warm.

Meanwhile, heat the clarified butter in a skillet over medium heat. Working in batches, add the prosciutto slices and cook until they are crispy, 5 to 6 minutes. Transfer to a paper-towel-lined plate and set aside. When the prosciutto is cool enough to handle, break it up into small pieces.

Preheat the broiler. Broil the salmon for 10 minutes for each inch of thickness on the fish until the skin is crispy and bubbly. To serve, place each fillet of salmon, skin-side up, in individual bowls. Sprinkle with the parsley leaves and pour ½ cup of the hot cider broth around each fillet. Garnish with the crispy prosciutto bits and serve.

Ricotta & Prosciutto-Stuffed Squash Blossoms

When I first moved to Italy, I thought Italians ate the strangest things—especially fried flowers. One taste of them, however, and I was converted. Fried squash blossoms are delicious even when they're empty, but filling them with ricotta and prosciutto only makes them better. These are best eaten as a passed snack: I like to stand at the stove as I fry them, passing them to guests as soon as they are done and encouraging them to eat the blossoms immediately. A lot of people say you shouldn't fry in extra-virgin olive oil, but in the Mediterranean everyone does it. I think it adds great flavor to the whole process and is well worth it. But don't use your expensive good stuff: Buy some decent bulk Italian or Greek oil for frying.

For the blossoms:

¼ cup diced prosciutto di Parma (if you have scraps, use them)

8 ounces fresh cow's- or sheep's-milk ricotta

1 egg, lightly beaten

½ cup grated Parmigiano-Reggiano cheese

2 tablespoons finely chopped parsley

Sea salt and freshly ground black pepper

24 small squash (such as zucchini) blossoms

For the batter:

1 cup all-purpose flour

1½ cups club soda or seltzer

3 cups extra-virgin olive oil, for frying

Coarse sea salt

serves 6 to 8

Stuff the blossoms: Puree the prosciutto in a food processor until it turns into a paste. Fold in the ricotta, followed by the egg, Parmigiano and parsley. Season with salt and pepper.

Fill a plastic bag with the prosciutto mixture. Snip off one corner and pipe 1 to 2 tablespoons of filling into each squash blossom—they should be full, but not bursting. Lay the blossoms out on a baking sheet and refrigerate while you make the batter.

Make the batter: Place the flour in a large bowl and whisk in the club soda or seltzer. Let the mixture rest 30 minutes to allow the flour to absorb all the water it can. After 30 minutes, check the consistency of the batter, adding a pinch more flour or a bit more soda if needed. The batter should be slightly thinner than Elmer's glue.

In a medium saucepan, heat the oil until it reaches 360° on a deep-fry thermometer. Dip each blossom in the batter, making sure it is well-coated, then transfer to the oil and fry. You can fry 2 to 4 blossoms at a time, but be sure not to crowd the pan and let the oil return to 360° before frying another round. Once the flowers are golden and crunchy and the batter is thoroughly cooked through, about 3 to 4 minutes, transfer the blossoms to a paper-towel-lined plate and sprinkle with coarse sea salt. Repeat with the remaining blossoms. Serve and eat immediately.

Prosciutto Scrap Ragù

In my restaurant, we always have prosciutto trimmings and scraps hanging around. Rather than throw them out, I like to use them up in frugal Italian farmhouse fashion by adding them to our meat ragù. Veal, which is mild and rather lean, makes a good bedfellow to the aggressive salt and fat content of prosciutto scraps. This is an all-purpose ragù, which we use for everything from simple dried pasta to laborious lasagna to a humble bowl of polenta.

If you don't have prosciutto scraps on hand, you should be able to find them at a good gourmet butcher shop that slices prosciutto in house; the shop should have prosciutto butts (the bottom of the ham where it shrinks down to a leg) available and will be delighted to sell them to you.

½ pound prosciutto di Parma butt or scraps, diced

1 onion, diced

2 celery stalks, diced

1 carrot, peeled and diced

4 garlic cloves, peeled

3 tablespoons freshly chopped herbs, such thyme, marjoram, sage and/or rosemary

2 tablespoons extra-virgin olive oil

2 tablespoons double- or triple-concentrate Italian tomato paste

Sea salt to taste

2½ pounds ground veal

1 cup white wine

makes 6 cups

Add the prosciutto to a food processor and process until it has formed a paste. Add the onion, celery, carrot, garlic and herbs to the prosciutto and process until you have a smooth puree.

In a large heavy-bottomed saucepan, heat the oil over low heat. Add the prosciutto and vegetable puree and a pinch of salt; cook until the mixture has darkened slightly in color and the fat has rendered from the prosciutto.

Dissolve the tomato paste in 1½ cups of lukewarm water, then add to the pot. Turn the heat up and cook briskly until the water is almost completely evaporated. Add the veal and stir vigorously with a wooden spoon. You are trying to make sure all the meat gets broken up nicely and doesn't form clumps. Add the wine and let it simmer to evaporate the alcohol.

Turn the heat to very low and cook the sauce slowly, stirring occasionally. If the mixture begins to stick to the bottom of the pan, add water in ½-cup increments. You want to cook this ragù as slowly as you can, ideally for about 4 hours, to meld all the flavors. When it's done, enjoy it with your favorite pasta or over soft polenta, or you can keep things simple and just spoon it over a piece of grilled bread. The ragù will keep three to four days in the fridge or two months in the freezer.

Tacos with Roasted Corn & Crispy Prosciutto

Working in New York City kitchens over the past 15 years, I've made plenty of nontraditional tacos as quick family meals for the staff. We generally use the ingredients we have on hand and tuck them in fresh corn tortillas brought from Staten Island or Queens by one of the cooks. In this version, I love to really toast and brown the corn, but be careful when you cook this because the corn can explode and pop.

¼ cup grapeseed oil, divided

4 ounces thickly sliced prosciutto di Parma, diced

3 shallots, finely chopped (about ¾ cup)

Kernels from 2 ears of fresh corn (about 2 cups)

1 fresh hot chile (such as jalapeño or Serrano), seeded and diced, (optional)

2 limes

8 to 10 corn tortillas, about 4 inches in diameter

½ cup crème fraîche

1 teaspoon Aleppo pepper

8 cilantro sprigs

serves ·4·

In a cast-iron skillet, heat 2 tablespoons of oil over low heat. Add the prosciutto and shallots and cook slowly until the prosciutto starts to crisp and the shallots are nicely wilted. Transfer the mixture to a plate, leaving as much fat in the pan as you can.

Turn the heat up to high and add the remaining 2 tablespoons of oil and the corn kernels. Cook, stirring frequently, until the corn starts to roast and pop. Let the corn get really caramelized. Add the fresh chile, if using. Turn off the heat and add the prosciutto and shallots. Cut one lime in half and squeeze the juice over the mixture. Keep warm. Cut the other lime into quarters and set aside.

Heat the tortillas directly over a gas flame until slightly blistered on both sides. Fill each taco with about 3 tablespoons of the prosciutto mixture. Garnish with a tablespoon of crème fraîche, a sprinkle of Aleppo pepper, a sprig of cilantro and serve with an extra lime wedge on the side.

Migas de Pastor

This humble Spanish dish—which is essentially bread fried with aromatics—exemplifies the Mediterranean tradition of extending leftovers. By adding a bit of meat to stale bread, you get a satisfyingly delicious snack. While I was testing this recipe at the restaurant, my chef kept stealing them to garnish his fried eggs. They're also great as a fancy version of croutons in a salad.

1 pound stale artisan bread, crust removed and diced into small cubes

1 teaspoon sea salt

6 tablespoons extra-virgin olive oil

serves **8**

4 garlic cloves, crushed

1¼ cups diced prosciutto di Parma

1 tablespoon smoked Spanish paprika (pimentón de la Vera)

¼ cup diced parsley

Cut the bread the day before you want to use it and place in a bowl. In a small bowl, combine ¼ cup of water with 1 teaspoon of salt and stir until the salt has dissolved. Sprinkle some of the salted water over the bread cubes, then let them sit overnight.

The following day, crumble the bread cubes with your fingers. Heat the oil in a cast-iron skillet over low heat. Add the garlic and prosciutto and cook slowly until the garlic just begins to brown. Add the breadcrumbs and paprika and fry until golden. When the breadcrumbs are fried and golden, stir in the parsley and let the mixture cook a few more minutes. Eat these within a few hours of preparing then.

Caldo Verde
with Prosciutto Bone Broth

Caldo verde is the national dish of Portugal. This classic kale and potato soup is enriched with a broth made from the prosciutto bone, a great flavoring agent that a frugal cook should never throw away. If you haven't purchased and used a whole prosciutto lately, you should be able to purchase a bone from a butcher or gourmet store if you ask nicely. The kale cooks down to a soft sweetness as the potatoes disintegrate and form a thick base.

---

1 prosciutto di Parma bone with most of the meat sliced off

8 cups chicken stock (preferably homemade)

¼ cup extra-virgin olive oil, plus more for drizzling

1 yellow onion, finely chopped (1½ to 2 cups)

1 small dried chile, such as chile de árbol

2 bunches kale, stems removed and cut into 1-inch ribbons

1½ pounds Yukon gold potatoes, peeled and cut into 1-inch cubes (about 3 potatoes)

Pinch of sea salt

serves 6 to 8

In a stockpot, simmer the prosciutto bone in about 5 to 6 cups of water for 5 to 10 minutes to get rid of some of the fat and scum. Discard the water and rinse off the bone.

Return the bone to the pot and cover with the stock. Bring to a simmer and cook gently for at least 45 minutes and up to 90 minutes, until the broth is nicely infused with the prosciutto flavor.

Meanwhile, in a large heavy-bottomed saucepan, heat the oil over low heat. Add the onion and cook, stirring, until it is translucent but not

browned at all. Add the dried chile and the kale. Cook, stirring, until the kale is wilted, then add the potatoes. Add the prosciutto broth and simmer slowly until the potatoes disintegrate and the kale is very well cooked, about 45 minutes. Taste the soup and season with a pinch of sea salt if you like—the prosciutto bone will have already given the broth a salty flavor.

Divide the soup among bowls, drizzle with oil and serve.

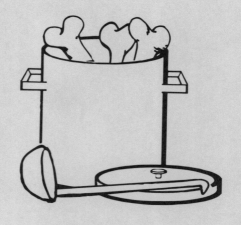

Thank You!

I'd first like to thank the Short Stack team for thinking of me for this book. I would also like to thank the lovely folks at the prosciutto di Parma *consorzio* for providing me with a delicious, beautifully aged ham to test my recipes.

I'd also like to thank my tireless staffs at Porsena and Porchetta for enabling me to do everything I want to achieve. Finally, I want to thank my son, Nadir Leander, for the joy he brings me every single day.

Share your Short Stack cooking experiences with us (or just keep in touch) via:

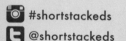 #shortstackeds

@shortstackeds

facebook.com/shortstackeditions

hello@shortstackeditions.com

Colophon

This edition of Short Stack was printed by Circle Press in New York City on Mohawk Britehue Ultra Lava(interior) and Neenah Oxford White (cover) paper. The main text of the book is set in Futura and Jensen Pro, and the headlines are set in Lobster.

Sewn by: W.E.

Available now at ShortStackEditions.com:

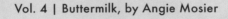
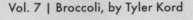
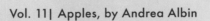